Eskimos – The Inuit of the Arctic

We call them Eskimos but they prefer to be known as the Inuit. Their story begins about 8,000 years ago when their ancestors arrived in Alaska from Asia. Hunting and travelling filled their lives in the coldest possible climate. They met together in summer camps to swop stories, play games and carve ornaments and weapons. This happy life was spoiled by the arrival of the Europeans who tried to seize their lands and wiped out the wildlife on which the Inuit depended for their living.

Gradually their lives have improved again and now they have their own lands, run their own schools and businesses and make their own laws. The Inuit can look forward to a happier future.

PEOPLE OF THE WORLD

INUIT

Anne Smith

People of the World

Aborigines
Inuit
Plains Indians

All words in **bold** are explained in the glossary on page 46.

Cover: An Inuit hunter on a skidoo, Baker Lake, Canada.
Frontispiece: The skidoo is a common form of transport for the Inuit.

This book is based on an original text by J.H. Greg Smith.

First published in 1989 by
Wayland (Publishers) Ltd
61, Western Road, Hove
East Sussex BN3 1JD, England

© Copyright 1989 Wayland (Publishers) Ltd

2nd impression 1991

Edited by Joan Walters
Designed by Ross George

British Library Cataloguing in Publication Data
Smith, Anne
    Inuit. – (People of the world).
    1. Eskimos
    I. Title II. Smith, J.H. Greg. Eskimos.
    III. Series
    970.004′97

    ISBN 1–85210–683–2

Typeset by Kalligraphics Limited, Horley, Surrey.
Printed in Italy by G. Canale and C.S.p.A., Turin

Contents

Who are the Inuit?   6
Chapter 1   The earliest Inuit   8
The Thule   10
Chapter 2   Life with the Inuit   12
Winter and spring hunting   12
Summer camps   14
The Inuit living together   16
**Chapter 3   Europeans come to
    the Arctic**   18
Looking for the North West Passage   18
Fur traders and whalers   20
Missionaries   22
Hungry times for the Inuit   24
Chapter 4   Trying to help the Inuit   26
Teaching the Inuit children   28
The discovery of oil and gas   30
Land claims in North America   32
The Inuit of Greenland   34
Chapter 5   The Inuit today   36
The modern Inuit world   36
The schools   38
A foot in two worlds   40
Back to the land   43
Chapter 6   The Inuit future   44

Glossary   46
Index   47

Who are the Inuit?

Many people call them **Eskimos** but their proper name is the **Inuit**. The word Eskimo means 'one who eats raw flesh'. Inuit means 'the people' and this is the name by which they like to be known. This book is all about the Inuit who live in the Arctic where winters are long, dark and very cold. Look at the map. The Inuit live mainly within the Arctic Circle, one of the coldest parts of the world.

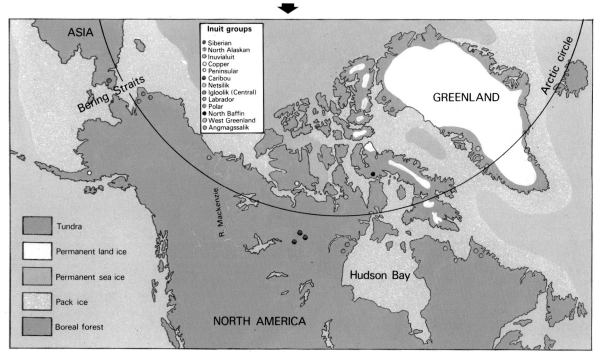

The Arctic is covered by snow for most of the year.
It is too cold for trees and plants to grow. The Inuit
used to build snow houses called **igloos**. They
trained dogs to pull sledges called **komatiks**.
Nowadays the Inuit live in houses like the ones in
this picture. They travel on sledges with motors,
called skidoos.

Chapter 1   The earliest Inuit

The first Inuit came from Asia to Alaska 8,000
years ago. You can see the route they took in the
map below. They hunted and fished for food. By
800 B.C. these people had settled in the Cape
Dorset area. We shall call them the Dorsets.

➤

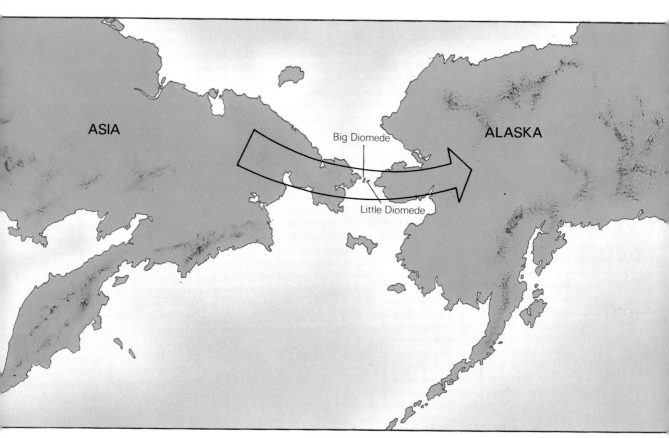

The picture carved on this comb made of bone
shows an archer and some of the animals he
hunted. The Dorsets hunted seals, walrus and
caribou. They made light sealskin canoes called
kayaks and lived in skin tents in the summer. In
the long cold winter they dug pits in the ground
and roofed them over with skins to make an
underground house. They heated these homes with
seal-oil lamps called **kudliks**.

The Thule

The Dorsets were replaced by the Thule, a group of clever, hunting Inuit. The Thule hunted walrus, caribou, seals and fish. They also hunted whales using kayaks and bigger boats called **umiaks**. These boats had a wooden frame covered with sealskin. The Thule liked to live together. They were brave hunters. A whale would give them meat to eat and oil for heat and light. The Thule lived in houses which they dug into the hillside near the sea.

Gradually the climate changed and it became colder. The waters where they hunted whales became blocked with ice. The Thule could not stay in one place any more and had to keep moving on. Very few groups were able to stay together.

The Thule used dogs to pull their sleds.

Chapter 2　　Life with the Inuit

Winter and spring hunting

The Inuit were always on the move. They carried
all they needed on dog-sleds. They needed skins
and furs for tents and bedding, cooking pots and
lamps, harpoons and knives for hunting, walrus
meat and **blubber** for food and dried grass to line
their boots.

➤

Inuit hunters walked many kilometres to catch seals.

In the winter seals live underneath the ice. They make a hole in the ice to breathe. Inuit hunters sit by the hole until the seal comes up and then spear it quickly with a harpoon. In spring seals live on top of the ice in the sunshine. This makes them easier to hunt.

Summer camps

In spring the sea-ice began to melt. The Inuit had
to move on to the land to camp. They were happy
in the summer because there was plenty of fishing
and hunting. They gathered berries and plants for
food too. They used kayaks and umiaks to hunt
seals and to travel to new camps.

The hunters killed the great musk ox for meat.
They also caught foxes, birds, squirrels and hares.
The summer was short and much time was spent
drying meat and fish to store as winter food.

The Inuit living together

Inuit groups liked to meet together at summer or winter camps. They had great feasts with music and **drum dancing**. They told stories which their grandparents had told them many years before. The Inuit played many special games. Two of these games are shown in the picture. The little boy tosses the bone and tries to catch it by putting his stick in one of the holes. The men are playing **finger pull**.

➡

At summer camp they liked to race, wrestle and toss each other in blankets. The Inuit children played all these games with the grown-ups.

Summer camp was a place for swopping stories, playing games and carving ornaments.

➤

The Inuit were happy people who loved their children and listened to old people's stories. Newborn babies were given special bracelets to help them be good at hunting or sewing. When someone died, they were dressed in their best clothes and furs and taken to a special place. The Inuit left them there for the wild animals to eat.

Chapter 3   Europeans come to the Arctic

Looking for the North West Passage

People believed that by crossing the north of
Canada they would find a short cut to China.
There, they could buy spices and become rich.
Martin Frobisher was an English sea captain.
He came to look for this North West Passage. The
picture shows the Inuit attacking Frobisher and
his men as they search for a way through the
Arctic ice.

The first Europeans to come to the Arctic were
Norsemen. They were unfriendly to the Inuit and
found their way of life too hard. The Norsemen
built homes and settled in Greenland.

Over the years
hundreds of
Europeans died
searching for the
North West Passage. ▶
Their ships had to
sail past icebergs in
the cold Arctic
waters.

Fur traders and whalers

Whalers came hunting in big ships like this. They were rough, greedy men who came hunting whales. They killed the bowhead whales for meat, oil and whalebone. Whalebone was used in ladies corsets. The whalers killed all the sea animals they could find. They did not like the Inuit but they gave them jobs. Soon there was not enough wildlife for the Inuit to hunt. Whalers brought unhappiness and sickness to the Inuit.

Many people in Europe wanted to buy furs. By 1821, the Hudson's Bay Company, which belonged to Britain, owned half the land of Canada. They had many trading posts like the one in this picture. The Inuit were not allowed to sell furs to anyone else. All the furs from Greenland went to Denmark, and Russia owned the trading rights in Alaska.

Missionaries

The work the missionaries did had both good and bad results.

ᑎᑎᕋᐅᓯᖅ ᓄᑖᖅ.
Titirausiq nutaaq.

ᐃ i	ᐅ u	ᐊ a	ᐦ H
ᐱ pi	ᐳ pu	ᐸ pa	ᑉ <
ᑎ ti	ᑐ tu	ᑕ ta	ᑦ C
ᑭ ki	ᑯ ku	ᑲ ka	ᒃ b
ᒋ gi	ᒍ gu	ᒐ ga	ᒡ L
ᒥ mi	ᒧ mu	ᒪ ma	ᒻ L
ᓂ ni	ᓄ nu	ᓇ na	ᓐ ᑌ
ᓯ si	ᓱ su	ᓴ sa	ᔅ ᒐ
ᓕ li	ᓗ lu	ᓚ la	ᓪ ᒄ
ᔨ ji	ᔪ ju	ᔭ ja	ᔾ ᒥ
ᕕ vi	ᕗ vu	ᕙ va	ᕝ ᒐ
ᕆ ri	ᕈ ru	ᕋ ra	ᕐ ᖅ
ᕿ qi	ᖁ qu	ᖃ qa	ᖅ ᖅ
ᖏ ngi	ᖑ ngu	ᖓ nga	ᖕ ᒐ
ᖠ ᶴi	ᖢ ᶴu	ᖤ ᶴa	ᖦ ᒐ

ᓈᓃᑦ NAANIIT

They saved the Inuit languages by writing them down. The picture shows how they wrote down one of the Inuit languages. When the Inuit were sick, they gave medicine to make them well. But the missionaries upset the old Inuit way of life. They would not let the children speak the Inuit language in school.

When missionaries came to live with the Inuit
they built churches and schools. These Inuit
are praying in a church in Greenland.

This church in Canada is built to look like an Igloo.

Hungry times for the Inuit

While people wanted to buy furs, the Inuit had money to live comfortable lives. From 1930 on, few people wanted furs and many Inuit starved to death. White men had brought illness to the Inuit. Many died of measles or influenza. This is an Inuit graveyard.

After the Second World War many Inuit worked
for the Americans on radar stations. These were
called Distant Early Warning Stations – the
D.E.W. line. These jobs did not last long. The Inuit
had no money again and no work. They had given
up their jobs as trappers and hunters.

Chapter 4   Trying to help the Inuit

Many people wanted to help the Inuit, but they did not always do what was best for them. They did not ask the Inuit what they wanted. Inuit groups were moved from their old homes to new ones many miles away, like this modern house built by the Canadian government.

➡

People tried to bring the Inuit together in new groups. In their old life the Inuit had lived with their own family group. This new life did not seem natural to them. They had schools and hospitals but no animals to hunt. They were unhappy, poor and sick.

Teaching the Inuit children

Inuit children in school were not taught in the language which their fathers and mothers spoke. They were often taken from their parents to live in schools many miles away. They did not learn the Inuit skills of hunting or trapping. Instead they learnt about the white people's life.

Many Inuit children became unhappy and behaved badly. They could not get jobs and were very poor. Some of them could not even talk to their parents. They wanted to be able to decide for themselves how they would live.

A Greenland town school.

The discovery of oil and gas

In 1968 oil and gas were discovered under the sea
in Alaska. Oil and gas finds would make
governments very rich. But it meant that many oil
wells were built out in the Arctic Ocean. To
transport the oil and gas, pipelines, like the one in
the picture above, had to be laid by digging up the
land. The Inuit were afraid that their lands, the
sea and the wildlife would all be destroyed. They
wanted Arctic nature protected. They stopped the
Canadian Government digging a pipeline to the
sea down the McKenzie Valley.

Land claims in North America

The Inuit believed that the land they lived on, belonged to them. They wanted governments to agree to this. If lots of money was made from oil or gas found on their land, the Inuit wanted a share. In 1971 the American Government gave 44 million acres of land in Alaska to the native Indians, the Aleut and the Inuit.

Inuit leaders meet to discuss plans for their people.

Inuit leaders meet a man from an oil company.

They also gave them 900 million dollars. With this
money they made jobs for the native people and
gave them training. The Inuit also began to set up
their own local governments. In 1982 the people of
North Canada voted to have their own Inuit
region. It will be called **Nunavut** which means
'our land'.

The Inuit of Greenland

The Inuit who lived in Greenland wanted to rule their own land too. They told the Danish Government that they wanted to live their own way of life. They did not want their children taught in Danish. By 1979 the Greenlanders had won their battle. Greenland is still part of Denmark but the Greenlanders have their own government. Nuuk is the capital of Greenland.

Jonathan Motzfeldt
(centre) is Greenland's first
Prime Minister.
The Inuit of Alaska,
Canada and Greenland
now have their own
newspapers and
television. They
make all their own
plans. Arctic nature
and wildlife is
protected and above
all, the Inuit
language is used.

An Inuit Conference

Chapter 5   The Inuit today

The modern Inuit world

A modern Inuit family lives in a wooden house.
They have central heating, a kitchen and a
bathroom. Most have television, radios and record
players. They watch the latest films on video
recorders. Snowmobiles or skidoos are used for
travelling and hunting. Aeroplanes come
regularly to even the most distant parts of the
land. The Inuit are all used to flying. Now they can
keep in touch with other Inuit all over the North.

◀ Inuit children playing video games.

The schools

Inuit schools have changed. Even the smallest group of Inuit have a school and a nursing station. The children are taught the Inuit language. In the spring and summer they are given time to learn about hunting and fishing with their families. If they are looking for caribou, they pull their komatik (sled) behind a skidoo. If they are fishing for **char** or trout they go out in a boat.

Hunting trips are happy times for Inuit children.
They are as important as going to school.

➡

A foot in two worlds

The Inuit who live in big towns cannot go hunting or fishing. The clothes that they wear are a mixture of their old and new ways of life. They usually wear jeans and sweaters with a parka on top. Their **mukluks** (boots) and their mittens will be trimmed with animal fur. Some of their clothes are bought in shops. Others are made at home. The Inuit make money by selling meat and fish, making clothes, carving and painting and working as tourist guides. But there are still not enough jobs for everyone.

This Arctic char is being cut up to be cooked. They ◗ travelled on the skidoo to catch it.

Sewing is a good job. ➡

Back to the land

It would be easy for the modern **Inuk** to forget old Inuit skills. Legends and stories told by grandparents and the games they played could be lost for ever. But now the young Inuit are being taught to hunt and trap. There are seal-skinning competitions and they still do blanket tossing and drum dancing. Many work on Inuit history projects. Dog teams are being raced for sport.

Times are still hard for some Inuit. They have no jobs and there are not enough teachers, and doctors. They hope that the future will be happier.

A modern Inuk catches a fish.

43

Chapter 6   The Inuit future

The Inuit will never leave the North now. They have seen many changes to their lands. Many Europeans are trying to stop seal hunting and fur trapping. This will affect the amount of money the Inuit can earn. Oil wells are being built in the Arctic. The Inuit are afraid that these will **pollute** the sea and harm the Arctic wildlife.

Inuit still sometimes use dog-sleds for transport.

Helicopters bring the modern world much closer.

They want their children to remember Inuit history, language and the old skills of hunting. But the children watch many television programmes made for Americans and Europeans. The Inuit are happy that their modern life is more comfortable. They will have to work hard to hold on to the skills and language of the old Inuit people.

Glossary

Blubber The fat of whales or other sea mammals.
Caribou A large deer which lives in the Arctic.
Char A fish like a large trout.
Drum dancing Men would beat on skin drums, while men and women danced. The beating and dancing got quicker and quicker.
Finger pull An old Inuit game played between two men. The first to give in was the loser.
Norsemen People from ancient Scandinavia (now called Sweden, Norway and Denmark).
Pollute To spoil, make dirty or poison.

Glossary of Inuit words

Eskimo An Indian word meaning 'eaters of raw flesh'.
Igloos Inuit houses made from blocks of snow.
Inuit An Indian word meaning 'the people'. This is the name by which the Inuit like to be known.
Inuk One Inuit person.
Kayak The Inuit sealskin covered boat.
Komatiks Inuit dog-sleds, now often pulled by skidoo.
Kudliks Lamps which were used for lighting and cooking. They burned whale oil or seal oil and had a moss wick.
Mukluk A boot made of sealskin or caribou. It was lined with moss to keep feet warm.
Nunavut An Inuit word meaning 'our land'. The Inuit will have their own region in Canada called Nunavut.
Umiak A large boat used by the Inuit to hunt whales.

Index

Aeroplanes 36
Alaska 8, 21, 31, 32, 35
Aleut, the 22, 32
Americans 25, 32, 45
Arctic, the 6, 7, 18, 19, 44
Asia 8

Blubber 12

Camps 14, 16
Canada 18, 21, 23, 31, 33, 35
Caribou 8, 10, 38
Children 16–17, 28–29, 34, 45
China 18
Churches 22–3
Climate 9, 11

Denmark 34
Dogs 7, 10, 12, 43, 44
Dorsets, the 8, 9, 10
Drum dancing 16, 23, 43

Europeans 18, 19, 45

Fish 10, 15, 39, 43
Fishing 8, 14, 38, 40
Food 8, 10, 12, 14, 15
Furs 12, 17, 21, 24, 40, 44

Games 16, 37
Gas 31, 32

Greenland 18, 21, 23, 29, 34, 35

Houses 7, 10, 26, 36
Hunting 7, 8–9, 10–11, 12–13, 14, 17, 20, 25, 28, 38, 39, 40, 43, 45

Igloos 7
Illness 24
Inuit lands 32–3

Jobs 20, 25, 29, 33, 40, 43

Kayaks 9, 10, 14
Kudliks 9

Languages 22, 28, 35, 38, 45

Missionaries 22–3
Music 16
Musk ox 15

North West Passage 18–19

Oil 31, 32, 44
   seal 9
   whale 10, 20

Radar stations 25
Russia 20

Schools 27, 28, 38–9
Seals 9, 10, 13, 14, 44
Sealskins 9, 10, 43
Skidoos 7, 36, 38
Sledges 7, 12, 38, 44

Thule, the 10–11

Umiaks 10, 14

Walrus 9, 10
Whalebones 20
Whales 11
   Bowhead 20
   hunting 20

Acknowledgements

The illustrations in this book were supplied by the following:

Brian and Cherry Alexander *Cover* and *Frontispiece*, 10, 36, 38, 40;
Arktisk Institut 17, 29; Committee for Original Peoples Entitlement
15, 31; Mary Evans Picture Library 20; Fagfotograf 35 (top); Werner
Forman Archive 9; Preben Kristensen 13 (top), 27 (top), 44; Mansell
Collection 14; Lars T Rasmussan 35 (bottom); J H Greg Smith 22
(bottom), 23, 24, 25, 26, 32, 33, 34, 37, 41, 42 (top and bottom); Topham
Picture Library 27, 28, 39, 43. The remaining photographs are from the
Wayland Picture Library. The maps on pages 6 and 8 were drawn by
Bill Donohoe and the illustrations on pages 11, 12–13 and 16 are by
Gerry Wood.